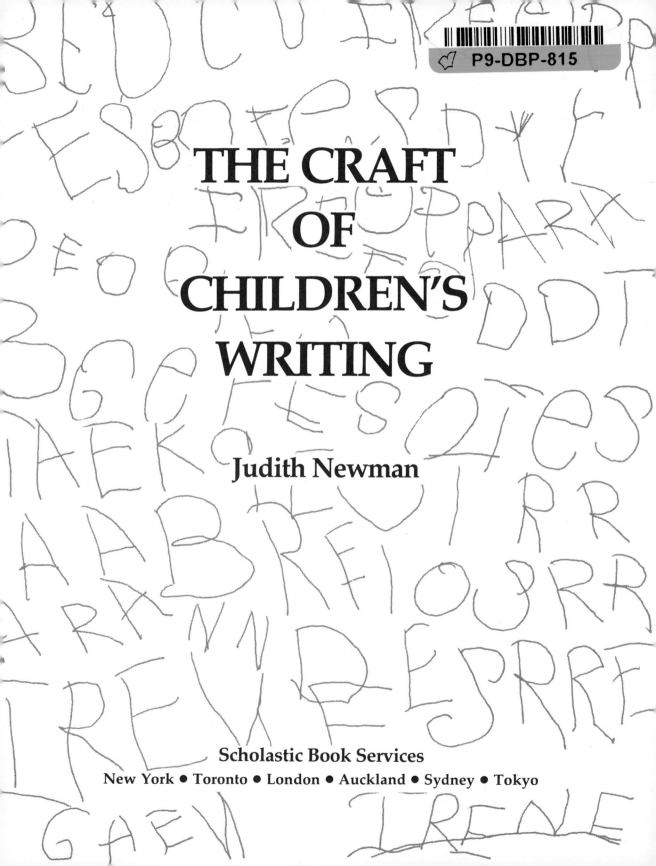

# THE CRAFT
# OF
# CHILDREN'S
# WRITING

### Judith Newman

**Scholastic Book Services**

**New York • Toronto • London • Auckland • Sydney • Tokyo**

## Acknowledgements

I wish to express my thanks to Jerome Harste, Carolyn Burke and Virginia Woodward. Their research on young children's reading and writing forms the basis of the theoretical framework I have used here for examining children's writing. Frank Smith's book *Writing and the Writer* was also important in helping me to understand the nature of the writing process.

I wish, too, to thank the children who willingly shared their work with me, and the teachers who provided samples of their children's writing. In particular, special thanks is due to Sheila Wainwright, Shawn's teacher. She experimented freely in her classroom and conscientiously collected writing from several children throughout the school year.

Special acknowledgement must go to the Social Sciences and Humanities Research Council for their support of the Beginning Literacy Project (S.S.H.R.C. Research Grant #410-80-0721R1). Several of the samples I have used were collected as part of that research effort.

**Cover photo by Barbara Campbell**

**Design by Annette Tatchell**

**1st printing 1984**          **Printed in Hong Kong**

Canadian Cataloguing in Publication Data

Newman, Judith Marta, 1943-
  The craft of children's writing

(Bright ideas)
Bibliography: p.71
ISBN 0-590-71449-X

1. Children as authors.    I. Title.

PN171.C5N48 1984      809'.89282      C84-098607-6

# Introduction

This is a letter to me from my friend Irene, a first-grader.

Dear Judith,
Can I go to Cabbagetown
and take Dori's place?
Love Irene

When I look at her letter I ask myself, What does Irene know about writing? I ask this question because we are used to looking at written language through conventional eyes; we are used to seeing what children don't know. At first glance, for example, I might see in Irene's letter what could be considered undeveloped fine motor control: her printing isn't well executed. I might see her misspellings, which initially make her message somewhat difficult to read. I could also notice an odd use of punctuation. All of these observations reflect a particular set of expectations about what children's writing should be like. We expect that the letters should be printed carefully and legibly. We expect conventional spelling, grammar and punctuation. Yet a closer look at Irene's letter forces us to examine our expectations, to question our beliefs about what is involved in learning to write.

What else do I see in Irene's letter? First of all, I see *intention*. Irene wants to communicate with me, and she has learned she can do that through a letter. Her purpose in writing is to ask if she can go with me for lunch at Cabbagetown (a restaurant) in place of Dori, who happens to be out of town. Knowing something of the situation makes Irene's letter more readable. Not only are her intentions clear, but she has selected an appropriate form — a letter — in which to express them.

In addition to intention, the letter demonstrates *organization*. It has a salutation, a body and a closing, as letters do. Irene has used other aspects of organization as well, which are too obvious for us to notice readily: she has written from left to right and from top to bottom, leaving spaces between words. Those spaces tell us that she knows about words. She has learned about upper and lower case letters: she uses a capital letter for the salutation and closing (*Der, Love*), for names (*Gud, Dori* and *Irene*), for the pronoun *I*, and for beginning a sentence (*And*). She has also organized what she wants to say grammatically. Her question 'Can I go to Cabbagetown and take Dori's place?' is grammatically acceptable.

We can see *experimentation* in Irene's letter too. Notice the periods separating the words. She has seen people use those punctuation marks and is trying them out for herself. Also notice what might well be an apostrophe in *Dor'i*. We can see a willingness to experiment with spelling. It is clear that Irene knows she knows how to write some words, and that she is unafraid to take risks with words she hasn't yet learned. Risk-taking is an integral aspect of experimenting. Learning to use what you have at your disposal, even though you know it isn't right, is an important part of learning to control the writing process. We can see that Irene has learned to do the best she can with what she has.

Another aspect of writing that we can see here is *orchestration*. A common belief about learning to write is that you need to master each part of the process in turn, to deal first with printing, then spelling, next punctuation, and finally form. In Irene's letter we are able to see how she deals with all facets of language at once. She considers the social, situational aspects of creating a piece of writing at the same time as she deals with decisions about meaning, spelling, grammar and punctuation. She is engaged in the complex juggling of pragmatic, semantic, syntactic and graphophonic aspects all at the same time.

We see evidence of this juggling in the overwriting of the e in *Der*, in the closing of the u in *Gud*, in her scratching out of *to* before *Dori*. We can see it in every spelling, punctuation and capitalization decision she makes. And most of all we can see it in the organization of the contents of her letter.

I have chosen this piece of writing, only thirteen words in length, to illustrate just how complex the writing process is, and to point out how much young children can know about it. I have found that these four concepts — *intention, organization, experimentation* and *orchestration* — provide a useful framework for looking at children's writing, and I would like to examine each of them in turn. Then I will present a case study to illustrate how they can be helpful for understanding a child's development over an extended period of time.

# Intention

The world in which our children live is filled with print. Show a three-year-old a *Texaco* logo and she says as she touches it that it means 'gas.' A two-year-old on a trip to the library asks why a particular exit sign is green (since in his community exit signs are usually red). A two-and-a-half-year-old walking down the street comments on the *No Parking* signs all along one side, then suddenly turns and asks, 'Why aren't there any *Yes Parking* signs?'

Such comments made by very young children give us glimpses into their understanding of the functions of written language. Young children learn very early that print in their environment has meaning. They quickly come to expect written language to be meaningingful, to relate in some way to the situation in which it occurs.

We shouldn't be surprised, then, to find intention behind their writing; scribbling that has intention is the rule rather than the exception. Not only can we see an intention to create meaning in the marks young children make on paper, when we look carefully at those marks, we can also recognize particular types of text. Children, it seems, connect content with form from the outset.

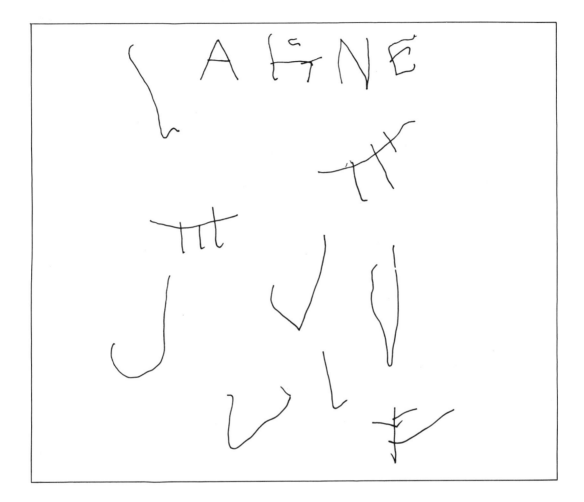

This piece of writing was done by Jane (age two years, nine months) the first time she was handed a paper and pencil. As we can see, the marks are recognizable as attempts at writing the letters of her name. She began by making the mark in the upper left corner, saying 'J' as she wrote it. Then she turned to me and asked me what came next. I wrote the A, which she attempted to copy. Next she offered me the pencil to help her write the rest. I returned the pencil to her, and with her hand in mine, we wrote N and E. The remaining marks she made herself.

Jane's intentions are clear. She has learned that names are represented by certain marks, marks she can recognize, and she uses this writing event to explore a meaning important to her: her own name.

Susan (age four) handed her mother a small piece of paper on which she had written:

> To Mommy,
> We all love her
> very much.
> Love
> Susan

Susan has learned that writing is done with letters of the alphabet. She uses the ones she knows, those which occur in her name, to represent her meaning. Susan's choice of paper size, the amount of writing and the way in which she lays it out are all strongly suggestive of a letter. It is probably not coincidental that the writing on the last line is very close to the spelling of her name.

Missing
water
in our
house.

This notice was prepared, with his mother's help, by Robbie (age four) one cold winter day when the pipes in his house had frozen. He wrote his notice with red magic marker on bright orange paper and taped it to the front door so that visitors would learn of the event when they arrived. His choice of words, the color of the pen and paper, the location in which he posted his sign all clearly show his intention.

It's tim to Put AwA
wit yis poing.

It's taime To come ovne
To The roG

It's time to put away
what you're doing.

It's time to come over
to the rug.

The children in one primary class made the discovery that it is possible to influence directly, through writing, what other people do. One day the children presented the teacher with several of these signs and told her that she didn't have to ask them to do things, she only needed to hold up their signs. Notice the choice of language, its layout on the page, the size and position of the accompanying drawings. All of these aspects demonstrate the children's awareness of what constitutes a poster.

Dear
Mrs. S.
Please
read
I'm Going
to
Run Away.
Love
Julie

Mrs. S. told her primary class that she had a very poor memory and that if they wanted her to remember something they would have to write notes to her. This note from Julie (age five) asks Mrs. S. to read *I'm Going to Run Away,* one of Julie's favorite books. Once again the appearance of the writing, the choice of paper (torn from a small notebook) and the language used all contribute to making Julie's intention explicit.

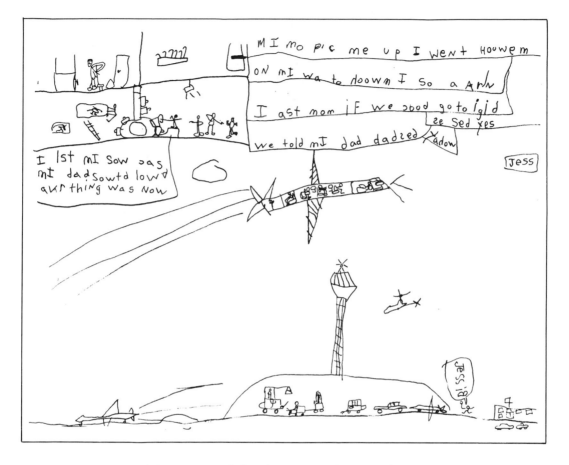

My mom picked me up. I went home.
On my way home I saw an airplane.
I asked mom if we could go to England.
She said yes.
We told my dad. Dad said, 'Yahow.'
I lost my suitcase.
My dad shouted loud.
Everything was new.

Jess (age six) chose to recreate his recent trip to England in the form of a cartoon. See how he places the language in relation to the pictures, including the balloon at the bottom of the page. Also notice how the text complements the illustrations.

From a very early age, young children expect written language to make sense. These examples show their amazing ability to coordinate the meaning they want to express with the form appropriate for expressing it. The notion that their scribblings are merely random marks on paper must, I think, be replaced by an understanding of how these early writing attempts are intentional efforts by the children to create and share meaning, using the tools they see the people around them using. Children are adept 'thieves.' They try out for themselves what they see working for others.

# Organization

Once we begin probing beneath the surface of children's writing, we immediately start to detect organization in what they produce. There are many aspects of organization to consider. To what extent, for example, does children's writing demonstrate an awareness of the conventions we have adopted for laying out writing on the page?

This is part of a ghost story written by Jane (age three and a half) one day while she was visiting me. To entertain her I handed her some paper and crayons with which to draw. Jane, however, wanted to 'make a book' instead. I expected her to dictate a story for me to transcribe, but she took the pencil I was holding and proceeded to write it herself. Fortunately for me, she composed out loud. Here is her story:

Mary Kate and Jane were playing outside.
Then they went inside to watch TV.
Then when they were watching TV
they saw a scary thing — a ghost.
So they hided under their covers.
Then the ghost couldn't see them.
The ghost felt sad
and he wrecked up the place.
Then the ghost finally leaved.
Then the girls lived happily ever after.

When Jane finished her story, she asked me to type it for her. We went to the typewriter and I asked her to read it to me. Her reading corresponded exactly to my transcription of what she had said as she wrote. In fact, when I tried to alter her text slightly she corrected what I was typing. She knew how she wanted her story to go. A couple of weeks later I had occasion to ask her to read her 'ghost book' to me. To my astonishment, her rendering of it still approximated the written text very closely.

Let's look carefully at what appears to be a page of scribbles. What strikes us immediately is the explicit horizontal layout of Jane's markings. As I watched her write her story, I noticed that she wrote from left to right, from top to bottom. Not only that, she had some sense of sentence. Each complete idea in her story was represented by a continuous mark.

There is another kind of organization in Jane's work as well. If we look closely, we can distinguish her drawing from her writing. The two ghosts on the left of the page have a different character from the marks she uses to represent text. Jane is clearly making decisions to use certain marks for writing — marks which are for the most part straight, horizontally arranged and connected — and other marks — circular and separated — for drawing.

There is also a sophisticated organization to her story, which contains many of the elements of a narrative. Her opening introduces the characters and places them in a setting. Then she provides a series of events involving an antagonist — the ghost. Finally, she ends with a resolution.

Dear Judith,
I have been waiting to go to Indiana, but we don't
have enough money. I have been missing you a
lot. I can read a lot now. I can spell YES. I
am having a great time for March Break. We went
to a brunch and it was sunny out. One night we
went to McDonald's. Gemma got me some ballet
slippers. Are you happy?
        Love Irene

Irene's letter (written about a year before her letter asking to join me for lunch at Cabbagetown) shows similar spatial organization features: she also writes from left to right, from top to bottom. What at first glance seems to be a random array of letters turns out, on closer examination, to consist of a narrower range of alternatives; we find *yes* and *Irene* (or parts of them) scattered throughout the letter. Irene has discovered that meaning can be represented by the rearranging of a finite set of symbols.

That was something Jane realized as well, shortly before she turned six. One day she turned to me and commented: 'Do you know something that really amazes me? The alphabet has only twenty-six letters and you get a whole language from that! Not only that, you get French too!'

While probably not able to articulate her discovery as clearly as Jane, Irene shows in her writing that she has understood the alphabetic principle of our writing system.

SRe. WOW
WBeq·and.
SRe. SOP
A WISHING·
WELL.

SRe. TOTO.
A. POPSN.
in. The.
WISHING.
WELL.
The. WISHING.
WELL.× SITO6.
OUCH.

She went
out and
she saw
a wishing
well.

She put
a penny
in the
wishing
well.
The wishing
well said
ouch.

These two pages from a story written by Irene almost a year later show several other organizational aspects. There is a definite segmenting of the text into words: she not only uses spaces, but as in her Cabbagetown letter, she separates words with periods. Notice how she judges how much to tell by the amount of space she has available to her.

Come home
now and
get some
hot
chocolate.

The organizational decisions Jane (age five) makes on this fifth page of a book she wrote are interesting. Having placed her drawing in the lower right corner of the paper, she has to figure out some way to represent the fact that the text consists of the words being spoken by the figure. She does that by electing to have it 'emerge' from the figure — which means that the writing has to be both backwards and from bottom to top, a convention we might have adopted in cartoons and one with which children frequently experiment. Jane creates another organizing device as well: she uses hyphens between words to show the connected nature of the speech.

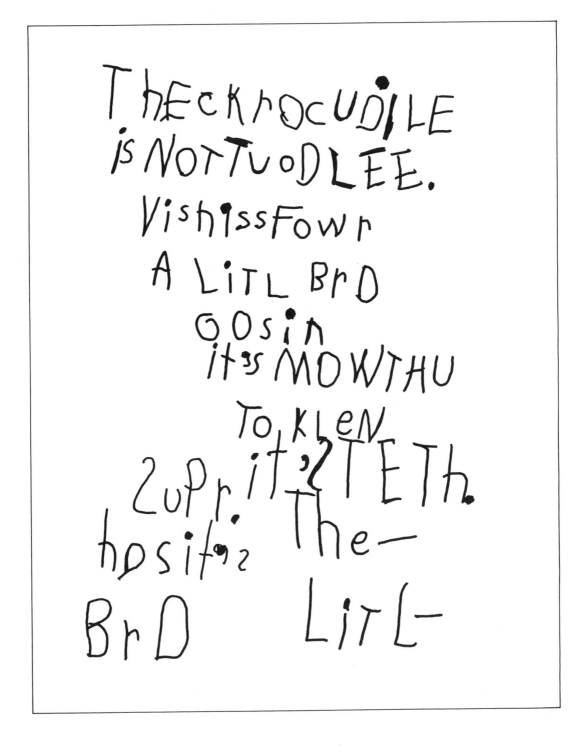

The crocodile
is not totally
vicious, for
a little bird
goes in
its mouth
to clean
its teeth.
The little
bird
has its
supper.

Jason (age six) elects to solve his organizational problem in somewhat the same way as Jane did. Having run out of room at the bottom of the page, he decides to use the space available at the lower left to finish his report, writing from bottom to top. He uses hyphens to indicate that more is coming and periods to indicate the end of an idea. The first period, which probably belongs after *vicious,* is possibly placed where it is because Jason believes that the end of a sentence occurs at the end of a line.

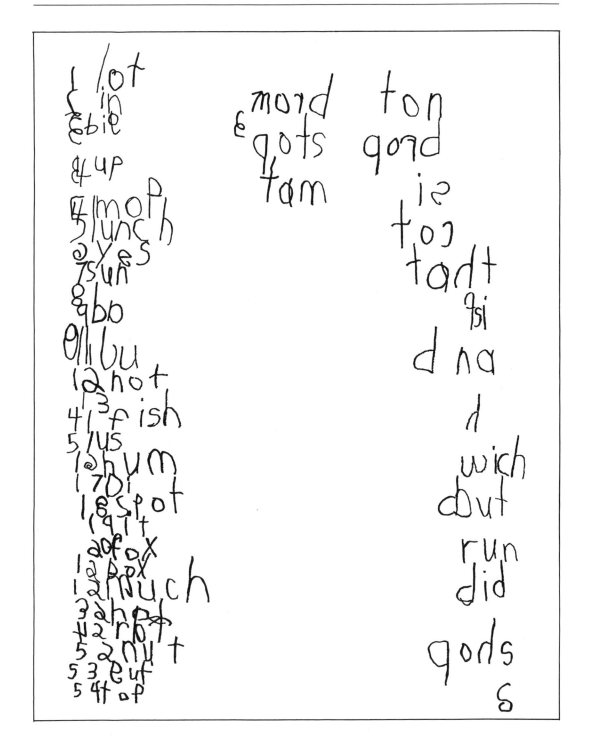

What organizing principle can we detect in this second-grader's spelling test? It seems that the child has a functional rule to help him format his list: write from the edge of the paper. Jimmy knows how to start his list on the top left, and the words on the left are, for the most part, written from left to right. But look at the words on the right: all but three of them are written in reverse, from right to left. When Jimmy runs out of space on the left-hand side of his paper, he writes on the other side, continuing to use his rule to 'write from the edge of the paper.' Hence, the majority of the words on the right are written backwards. What is amazing is the degree of control this child has, to be able to write backwards while retaining the within-word relationships. In some respects his sense of how the words look is more complex than ours. How many adults can write equally well forwards and backwards?

Organization pervades all children's writing. We can see that children make decisions about what they want to write. They select the appropriate form for their meaning and organize what they want to say so that it reads like a narrative, a letter or a report. And they make organizational decisions about how to format their writing on the page. These decisions demonstrate children's awareness of a large number of the conventions used for writing.

# Experimentation

A fundamental aspect of all language, whether spoken or written, is experimentation. Each time we speak or write we create language appropriate for a specific context. Although all of us, adults as well as children, are experimenting with language all of the time, we are more aware of the experiments children are conducting. The following comment by Michael (age two and a half) is typical. Michael was walking to the park with his mother. Ahead of them was an orange flashing light signaling a crosswalk. Michael turned to his mother and commented: 'That light is blowing kisses at me.'

Michael used what might be considered a complex metaphor to convey his meaning. Using what language he had at his disposal, as well as his knowledge of the world, he created a unique, yet apt, description of the situation. And his experiment brought a confirmation that his experience could, indeed, be described as he'd described it.

Young children experiment with spoken language from the moment they realize they can command attention by making noises intentionally. They experiment in the same way with written language.

·One morning Michael (age two and a half) sat down with a crayon and paper and carefully made these marks from left to right on his page. Then, putting down the crayon and pointing to each of his marks (also from left to right), he read in a book-reading voice: 'This says Michael.' It is tempting to speculate about the *M*-like and *A*-like marks. Their letter-like quality was probably accidental, but Michael's experimenting with writing wasn't.

Somewhere around her fourth birthday Jane began experimenting with letter/sound relationships. This particular piece was done one day as she watched me and her older brother Robbie writing at the kitchen table. We were playing with puns. Robbie (age six) had discovered that words have multiple meanings and he was having fun playing with this notion. He had, for example, drawn a picture of a cow, clothed it like a boy and then written *Cowboy* beneath his drawing.

Jane observed us for a while, then decided to get into the act herself. She quickly drew her picture, then sat for a moment with an intense look on her face. She looked at me and asked, 'How do you write Kentucky Fried Chicken?' I suggested she try writing it herself. She covered her face with her hands and said 'Tucky' several times, emphasizing the *t* at the beginning of the word as she said it. Finally she looked up, said 'T' and made a *T* just above the chicken's outstretched leg. Then she tried again. Once more she covered her face with her hands and repeated 'Tucky,' this time emphasizing the end of the word. She repeated the word several times before lifting her head and asking whether she needed a *c* or a *k*. I asked her which she thought it was. 'C,' she replied and proceeded to write a couple of them scattered on the page. Next she tackled *Fried*. Using the same procedure, hands over face and saying the word to herself several times, she was able to come up with *F* and *R* (on the far left, 'with its legs tied together'). *Chicken* was difficult. Jane struggled with the initial sounds, then settled for writing *CK* (the *H*'s) and a couple of *N*'s (which look like *W*'s).

While Jane's previous writing (remember her ghost story written at age three and a half) had shown an awareness of the linearity of writing, her concern with identifying letter/sound relationships on this occasion overrode whatever else she knew about writing. The letters went anywhere on the page; their formation was haphazard. Yet none of this seemed to detract from her sense of accomplishment when she had finished her effort and given it to me to keep.

Dear
Judith,
Are you
going to bring
me a present?

Daniel (age 5) wrote me a letter as I was leaving to return home from a visit to his family. At first he was reluctant to write anything on his own.

'How do you spell *dear*,' he asked his mother, who was sitting nearby.

'Do the best you can. You know Judith likes you to do it by yourself,' she replied.

'Does it start with *D*?' Daniel persisted.

'Write that down,' she answered him.

Daniel's insecurity persisted for quite a while. Before he would risk writing something, he would check with his mother. In response to each query, she encouraged him to write what he thought he wanted. By the

Have a nice time.
Love Daniel

Goodbye

time he reached the bottom of the first page he was experimenting more comfortably, and he completed the letter without further requests for help.

Why the reluctance to write? we might ask ourselves. Part of the answer, I think, can be found in Daniel's recent writing experiences. During the preceding six months he had come to understand his Kindergarten teacher's expectations for writing: that it be neat and accurate. Unlike Jane, who experimented without hesitation, Daniel had come to feel vulnerable about writing. Even though he was writing to an adult he knew well, one he knew would accept what he produced on his own, he was still reluctant to take risks. He resorted initially to one of the two strategies left to him: either ask someone or avoid writing altogether. Not until his mother demonstrated her support of what he tried did he elect to write by himself.

I. WS SC yastr day and
i cat ha cm tolw scow
I WSt MStr rs d ug

Was your brother sick at home
yesterday? no

I was sick yesterday and
I could not come to school.
I watched Mister Dress-Up.

This journal entry was written by Shawn (age 6) in mid-November. It is typical of his writing during that period. While willing to copy when he entered first grade, he was reluctant to write anything on his own. His teacher had persistently encouraged him to experiment by responding only to his messages. By mid-November Shawn's journal entries consisted of approximately fifteen words and he was no longer anxious about using words for which he didn't know the spelling.

In this particular entry he spelled only six of the sixteen words correctly (if we accept the lower case *i* in the second line). But when we look closely, we discover that most of what Shawn has written is partially correct. His 'errors' are largely omissions, and his spelling strategies are in fact quite well developed. He spells 'the way it sounds' and is able, for the most part, to identify the consonants he wants and place them in correct order. He also spells 'the way it articulates' (*scow* for *school*) and 'the way it looks' (*tow* for *two*). He has learned something about vowels. He has a preferred one — *a* — which he uses when in doubt. Shawn has learned to be a risk-taker with writing, experimenting comfortably in order to say what he wants to say.

---

A vital part of becoming a successful language user is being comfortable with the 'messing around' that must go on. In other words, experimentation is essential for learning language. Every spoken exchange, each writing effort, represents an experiment: Is this what I mean to say? Do I say it this way or that? Are these the particular words I want to use? Consequently, learning to be a successful language user is a risky business.

Yet if no risks are taken, little can be learned. One doesn't learn language as a watcher from the sidelines; one has to be a participant in what's going on. Expecting children to produce exact, correct language, whether oral or written, places unnecessary pressure on them as language users. When the cost of making mistakes becomes too great, children cease taking risks. This effectively removes them from the language arena since, as non-participants, their opportunities for learning are few. Children need to be able to experiment with what they want to say, to whom they want to say it, and how they want to say it. They need to experiment with form and format, spelling and punctuation. Learning to be a writer involves the refinement of many aspects of the process at the same time. That refinement comes about as a consequence of experimentation.

# Orchestration

Orchestration is another important notion to consider when looking at children's writing. What do I mean by orchestration? I'm referring to the complex decision-making that must go on in the process of creating any language, but particularly in creating a piece of writing. To begin, I (the writer) must have some general intentions; that is, I need to have narrowed the field to some topic, made some decisions about who the audience will be, and formed some notions about what I want to say. These general intentions are translated into more focused intentions as soon as I begin to consider how I am going to say what I think I want to say, and opt for some format in which to say it. Will this be a letter, a poem or a report of some sort? As I begin to write, I have to keep in mind my overall intentions while struggling with choice of words, spelling, sentence structure, punctuation. I have to experiment as I organize. I have to take risks as I muster my resources and try to make the whole thing work. And I mustn't loose sight of my audience while I'm working to get the marks on the page.

We know from the things young children say that they are capable of just such sophisticated orchestration. 'More booking please,' says Jessica (age two) as she hands me a favorite book she wants me to read to her. 'Those trucks don't have any faces,' comments Michael (age two and a half) as he surveys a row of truck trailers without their cabs. 'Don't you want to talk to Donna for a few hours?' Matthew (age four) asks his mother when she arrives to take him home from a birthday party he's enjoying. These are demonstrations of the complex decision-making of which young children are capable in the process of producing language. Using what language resources they have available, together with their sense of what a particular situation involves, they create language uniquely appropriate for specific contexts.

So, too, with their writing.

> DeAR MRSS MORRSiN
> Th'is      is ABotemichAel
> he is Sike
>
> MichAel
>
> ~~is is~~ is Sike

Dear Mrs. Morrison,
This is about Michael.
He is sick.
Michael is sick.

This note was brought to Mrs. Morrison one morning by a friend of Michael's. As the note informed her, Michael (age five and a half) was sick and wouldn't be in school that morning. We can see some of the complex decision-making that went into writing this note. Michael is aware that his absence might call for some explanation, so he decides to let his teacher know why he isn't in school. The fact that he uses an old paper bag shows his awareness of the informality permitted with note-writing. The words he chooses and the way he organizes what he says are very like what his mother might write in a note. He begins to say that Michael is staying home (see the words crossed out at the bottom of the note), but perhaps unsure that he can write all of that, he decides to repeat the fact that he is sick. Throughout, we see him orchestrating the decisions about how to represent the meaning he wants to communicate.

FEB 26 1981

TOdAY itisArAiNY bAy. What do you
like to do on rainy days? SAlAs inthe
PATl. Slushing in the puddles sounds
like fun!Yes

Today it is a rainy day.
(What do you like to do on rainy days?)
Slush in the puddles.

These two journal entries were written by Brian (age five and a half). In his primary classroom, the teacher and children used their journals to engage in written dialogues with one another. In the first sample we see that the teacher responds to what Brian writes by asking him a question and by commenting on the information he has provided. Look what happens a week later. Notice how Brian changes the nature of the

MAR 3 1981

TODAY It is A Good bAy to (@ to
The Bech to PlA in the sAd and toshm
and have SAM FUN WAd you like
toCM to. Yes please. I'll bring
some food.

Today it is a good day to go to
the beach to play in the sand and to swim
and have some fun. Would you like
to come too?

dialogue by ending his entry with a question for the teacher. Notice also his indirect way of saying that it's a nice day. While maintaining a focus on meaning, he controls sentence structure and makes decisions about what words to use, using some he knows how to spell, finding others around the room, and electing to do the best he can with the rest.

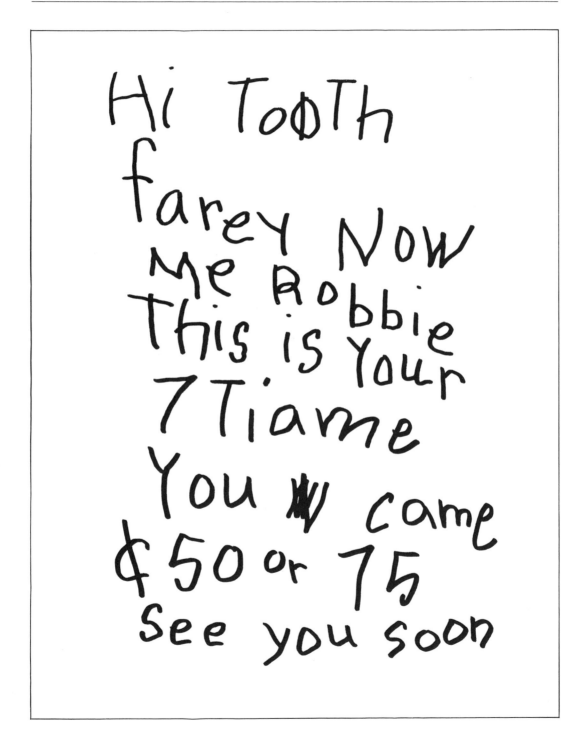

Hi Tooth
Fairy. Know
me, Robbie?
This is your
7th time
you came.
(I would like) 50¢ or 75.
See you soon.

This note, which Robbie (age seven) left under his pillow, is an intricate negotiation with the tooth fairy. He sets the context with a greeting, then introduces himself, reminding her that she should remember him (after all she's been there six times before). Next he tells her what he thinks this tooth is worth. Finally he closes informally. In the process of sustaining this negotiation, Robbie changes his mind about the spelling of *tooth*, and whatever it was he started to write before deciding on the word *came*. We see him choosing the symbol for cents rather than writing it out. We see him experimenting with capital letters for the beginnings of words. In writing his letter, Robbie draws upon and orchestrates his knowledge of informal letters, his prior experiences with the tooth fairy, his knowledge of how to use language persuasively and his sense of sentence structure, spelling and punctuation.

The HAUNTED.HouSE
ONe dark aNd StorMY
Night I caMe uPoN
A hauNted house
ANd aPuF.A WichbcaMe
Aot ANd trNdM
iNTO A Fragle ANd
I tRid to
Go. BAt the Wich
Put Me iNto.A
KAg She got the
KtL Rety FoR Me
to BEE iN the souP

The Haunted House
One dark and stormy
night I came upon
a haunted house
and poof, a witch came
out and turned me
into a frog and
I tried to
go. But the witch
put me into a
cage. She got the
kettle ready for me
to be in the soup.

Chapter two
The witch put me
in the kettle
and that
was the end
of me but her
cat ate me up and
my dad couldn't
find me.

Janel (age six) began her story by borrowing an introduction from a book in the classroom; hence the conventional spelling in the first four lines, at which point she launched into a narrative of her own. In her title we see Janel using a period to separate the words *Haunted* and *House*, which she happened to print too closely together. She uses this strategy after *puf, trnd* and *into* as well. Notice, however, that the period after *I trid to go* is probably marking the end of a sentence.

Let's look at Janel's spelling strategies. She has control of the conventional spelling for many of the words she wants to write. Of the forty different words she uses in her story, twenty-five (62.5%) are spelled conventionally. Her self-correction of *two, that* and *her* reveal the close interplay between reading and writing that Janel is able to manage. She knows how these words should look and changes them when she inadvertently spells them functionally. A close look at the words she does spell functionally reveals several strategies at work.

| Janel's spelling | Conventional spelling |
| --- | --- |
| *puf* | poof |
| *wicb, wich* | witch |
| *aot* | out |
| *trnd* | turned |
| *frag* | frog |
| *trid* | tried |
| *bat* | but |
| *kag* | cage |
| *ktl, ketl* | kettle |
| *rety* | ready |
| *bee* | be |
| *captr* | chapter |
| *av* | of |
| *mi* | my |
| *cudit* | couldn't |

Most of these words have been spelled the way they sound, a few the way they articulate (*rety, aot*). Her first spelling of *witch* (*wicb*) was probably a slip of the pen (*b* for *h*), since she subsequently spells it *wich*. She reconsiders *ktl,* which becomes *ketl* later in the story. She also has a sense of word length: *cudit* and *captr* look about right. Janel, then, uses several kinds of knowledge to help her represent what she wants to write.

Danielle, tell me about what you do in gymnastics. I do back hnsprings and rodofs and back wacovrs on beam. I bet back-walkovers on the beam are hard. How do you do them? I poTe mY hans and arms up and band backwrds sT-and like I am in a handsand and spliT mY lags opin Than poTe one lag done Than iT. The aThr and I lad iT. and I also do the splis.

(Danielle, tell me about what you
do in gymnastics.)
I do back
handsprings and roundoffs
and back walkovers
on the beam.
(I bet back-walkovers on the beam are
hard. How do you do them?)
I put my hands
and arms up and bend backwards,
stand like I am in
a handstand and
split my legs open,
then put one leg
down, then the other
and I land it. And I
also do the splits.

This written conversation with Danielle (age six) occurred during a videotaped interview. She had read a book for me and I had offered her some paper on which to write. She looked at me and said, 'Ask me something.' I replied, 'What would you like me to ask you?' to which she answered, 'About gymnastics.'

I began, then, by writing, 'Danielle, tell me about what you do in gymnastics.' She immediately wrote *I do*, then stopped and indicated that she didn't know how to spell what she wanted to write next. 'Just do the best you can. Don't worry about it,' I encouraged her. She resumed, saying very slowly and softly to herself what she was writing on the paper: *back hn* (pausing) *springs* (reading 'back handsprings,' then 'and') *and* (without mouthing the word) *rodofs* (saying the word to herself as she wrote it, then reading 'and roundoffs') *and* (again without saying the word) *bach* (saying it slowly as each letter was formed, then stopping, looking at *bach* and changing the *h* into a *k* by adding a stroke to it) *wacovrs* (once again slowly saying the word as she wrote it) *on beam* (saying 'beam' as she wrote).

Danielle then handed the paper back to me and I continued: 'I bet back-walkovers on the beam are hard. How do you do them?' She paused to think for a moment, pen in her mouth, then wrote: *I* (commenting 'Oh, oh,' putting a period after *beam* three lines back, then writing again) *pot* (saying the word 'put' softly to herself). As she finished the word she turned to me and said, 'That spells *pot*.' 'What do you want it to say?' I asked her. Without hestitation she added an *e* to the end: *pote*. 'There,' she said and continued writing *my* (silently).

This brief transcript provides a glimpse into the writing process. We see this young writer establish global intentions before writing, then confidently launch into her text, keeping track of many things at once. We see her using what she knows about her topic, about language, about spelling, taking risks and experimenting when she's not sure, concerned primarily with maintaining the flow of meaning. We see her functioning as a reader, making adjustments, correcting spelling, adding punctuation, keeping track of the organization of the event she's describing.

---

# Conclusion

Danielle's writing, perhaps most clearly of all, demonstrates the interconnectedness of *intention, organization, experimentation* and *orchestration*. While each of these language strategies has been discussed separately, I want to emphasize that they occur in concert. In Danielle's writing we are aware of the complex transactions that must take place in the process of producing a text.

Writing is not just a matter of learning to print, to spell words or to use punctuation. It requires the intricate and sophisticated orchestration of many different kinds of knowledge all at the same time. And as we have seen through these writings, even very young children have a sense of what is involved in the process. While children may use unconventional surface representations, their texts reveal definite semantic intentions, a focus on meaning, and an understanding of the relationship between language and language structure and whatever marks they choose to represent or 'place-hold' meaning.

As experienced language users, they know there is too much to orchestrate initially to make correct writing their goal. Instead, young children experiment freely, selecting from available resources what seems appropriate and/or interesting to try. They search for, find and represent text in exactly the ways that older, more experienced writers do. In order to appreciate children's writing development, then, we must be aware of the complex orchestration each end-product represents.

At this point it might be helpful to examine the writing of a single child done during one school year to see how these four concepts — *intention, organization, experimentation* and *orchestration* — provide a framework for understanding the intricacy of the learning-to-write process.

# Shawn: a case study

Shawn (age six) entered first grade after a difficult primary year. He hadn't liked going to school and had resisted doing school work. He was not reading much environmental print (that is, the writing on signs, packages, TV, etc.), nor was he reading from books, and while he was able to copy, he refused to write anything on his own. In his first-grade classroom, however, the teacher emphasized meaning. She never 'marked' the children's efforts, but responded to the meaning of their writing. Spelling and punctuation were not taught formally. Instead, the children were encouraged to write freely. Shawn's writing development in this supportive environment offers us many insights into writing development generally.

Shawn

Today is the first day of school. We made a house and read a books. We have 19 people in our class.

Good Shawn! Can you draw a picture to go with your story?

Today is the first day of
school. We made a house
and read a book. We have
19 people in our class.

This is Shawn's first journal entry, copied from the board on the first day of school. Together the class produced this news item, which the teacher wrote on the blackboard. The children were given notebooks and invited to create a news story of their own, but they were told they could copy the story from the board if they wished. Shawn elected to copy.

From this entry, we can see that Shawn knows how to write his name; he knows how to form the letters of the alphabet (even though the *p*'s in *people* are reversed); he has some sense of words, since he's left spaces between them; he has copied the punctuation appropriately. The word *in* (on the last line), with the upper case *N* written backwards, suggests that Shawn might have written that word from memory. The erasures are evidence that, although unable to name all of the letters of the alphabet, Shawn has visual skills sufficiently well developed to allow him to keep his place while copying text.

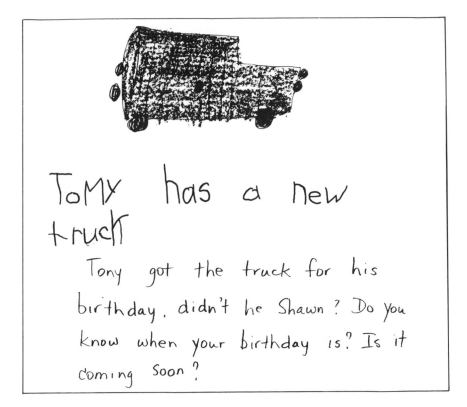

ToMY has a new truck

Tony got the truck for his birthday. didn't he Shawn ? Do you know when your birthday is? Is it coming Soon ?

Tony has a new truck.

This journal entry, written during the third week of school, is Shawn's first writing on his own. On the surface he doesn't appear to be much of a risk-taker; of the five words he's written, four are spelled conventionally. We can see editing for space (between *a* and *new*) and for spelling (*truck*) — further indication of his concern for what he's learned about convention. Yet for the first time Shawn was willing to generate his own message and in the process, while playing it safe, was able to find the words he needed from somewhere in his environment — evidence of his using reading for writing. Most important, his choice of words was determined by what he wanted to say, not by what he could spell.

His teacher's response, read to him as it was being written, was her attempt to draw Shawn out, to encourage him to write more. Shawn didn't answer her questions. Five words written on his own was the most he was willing to risk on this occasion.

*my Father ct a prtr*
*he Fat it in the grenhs*
What did your father do with the
partridge he caught in the
greenhouse Shawn?
*We lat it go*

My father caught a partridge.
He found it in the greenhouse.
(What did your father do with the
partridge he caught in the
greenhouse Shawn?)
We let it go.

By early October Shawn had become more comfortable experimenting with written language. We can see here that he is making definite decisions about which words he will look for (*father*) and which he will spell functionally (*ct, prtr, Fat, grenhs* and *lat*). The fact that certain words he wants to use are not readily available, either from books or from the writing around the room, doesn't prevent him from representing, or place-holding, his intended meaning as best he can. We can notice how he's begun to orchestrate meaning with letter/sound correspondences. Vowels have crept into some of his words. Some words (*my, he, it, in, the, we, go*) he has either learned to spell or is now able to find fairly easily. This is also the first time Shawn replied to the teacher's question. Notice how she used his words in her response. She did that so she would be able to read his journal entry later.

las nat at was halloween
I wt to 20 haos
What was your favorite
treat that you got last night?
chlabrs I lat

Last night it was Hallowe'en.
I went to 20 houses.
(What was your favorite
treat that you got last night?)
Chocolate bars I like.

Shawn is now experimenting freely. Notice the word *halloween*. The absence of a capital for *h* suggests that he began writing the word before looking for it in the classroom. The two inverted *e*'s also suggest that he didn't need to attend too closely to the word as he copied it. Seven of his twelve spelling decisions now result in functional spellings; his strategies include spelling the way it sounds (*las* for *last*, *nat* for *night*, *wt* for *went*, *chlabrs* for *chocolate bars*), spelling the way it articulates (*haos* for *house*), using another known word (*at* for *it*), and place-holding meaning (*lat* for *like*). Notice also the absence of spacing between words in his answer to the question. In his effort to orchestrate meaning and spelling, he forgets to worry about word spacing — an important indication that Shawn is becoming more relaxed with writing.

I WS SC YaS4r day and
i cdt na cm tow scow
I WSt MStr rs a u9
Was your brother sick at home
yesterday?no

I was sick yesterday and
I could not come to school.
I watched Mr. Dress-Up.

By mid-November Shawn was clearly focusing on the meaning of what he wanted to say. Words spelled conventionally in earlier entries are now spelled functionally (*ws* for *was, i* for *I*). He is writing much more, with less effort. In this entry he has three main ideas, concisely presented.

I haq my father cas
a dar fr as.
Chrr ws las af nsni
awr cisrm

Who was making all the noise
in our classroom? Chm gas.

I hope my father catches
a deer for us.
There was lots of noise in
our classroom.
(Who was making all the noise
in our classroom?) Them guys.

This journal entry, written in early January, is interesting for several reasons. The percent of conventional spelling is the lowest of any in Shawn's journal entries (21%). Yet at the same time we can see him experimenting with several new conventions. In addition to beginning each new sentence on a separate line (which he seems to have been doing consistently up to this point), he is now using periods to mark the end of some of his sentences. He also demonstrates an awareness of digraphs: *chr* for *there*, *chm* for *them*. In this entry Shawn edits for meaning in the process of writing (an indication that he is reading his own text): *ni* (*in*) is written over an erased *a* (the start of *awr* for *our*). The spelling of *in* (*ni*), *of* (*af*) and *our* (*awr*) are also of interest; they reveal that, in addition to his other spelling strategies, Shawn is 'spelling the way it looks.'

Ba Fr I wat to Scol
I Mad four Bag Sow
Bais to Mac a SowMall
and I halP the Saw
bds at Mlat Sa I
So I can hav May
Sow Man

I hope your snowman doesn't
melt either Shawn! What will you
do if it does melt? I Wal Balb
a nat r

Before I went to school
I made four big snow
balls to make a snowman,
and I hope the snow
doesn't melt so I
(so I) can have my
snow man.
(I hope your snowman doesn't
melt either Shawn! What will you
do if it does melt?) I will build
another.

By mid-February Shawn's journal entries are consistently longer (from the end of January to mid-April they average twenty-nine words) but they are still difficult to interpret; without the teacher's response we might be unable to read what he wrote. However, a close look at this text shows his continuing experimentation: *scol* is beginning to look decidedly like *school*; *four* is spelled conventionally; *sa* becomes *so* on the next line; he is developing a sense of the syllabic nature of words (*ba fr* for *before*, *bas at* for *doesn't*); every word but one (*fr* in *before*) now has a vowel (his preferred vowel is still *a*); and *p*, initially written backwards, is self-corrected (that is, Shawn noticed the incorrect orientation of the *p* and changed it on his own without any teacher intervention).

Of particular interest is the complexity of the grammar of what Shawn has written. He begins with a pre-positioned adverbial clause (*before I went to school*) and uses a subordinating conjunction to introduce a clause of reason (*so I can have my snowman*).

march 11

I todyu is Tuesday
I mst the Bus
todby and I gat
a driv to the scool.
I gat a driv by
mrss Mar bcs my
mtr don't have the car.
Why did you miss the bus at
the bus-stop Shawn? because
I dent her the BUS

March 11,
Today is Tuesday.
I missed the bus
today and I got
a drive to the school.
I got a drive by
Mrs. Mar because my
mother doesn't have the car.
(Why did you miss the bus at
the bus-stop Shawn?) Because
I didn't hear the bus.

A sophisticated orchestration is evident in this journal entry. Shawn coordinates his meaning intentions with information he selects from around the classroom; he organizes his text; he uses his growing store of conventional spellings, at the same time experimenting with a range of functional spelling strategies. This journal entry was the first occasion Shawn chose to date his writing. Notice his use of the comma after the *11* in the date. Notice also his spelling of *tody* in the first line (no capital *t*, the *a* omitted), a word now written on his own. *Driv, mrss* and *don't* are words he's seen before. His insertion of the *u* in *scuol* in the process of writing reflects his coordination of reading and writing. Most interesting is his spelling of *because* (*bcs* in the body of the text, *because* in the response to the teacher's question) and *today* (*tody* followed by *today* two lines below). His use of a functional spelling followed by a conventional one demonstrates the kinds of decisions Shawn is making in the process of writing. While he either knows how to spell the word he wants or knows where to find it easily, he elects to place-hold the meaning in the first instance, using a functional spelling in order to get his meaning down — an important, and necessary, writing strategy.

Monday' March 24

I went to niy nies
and arin cut his had
and my father cut
his tow wah the
Piwr_si

Did your father have to have.
Stitches in his toe. Shawn? Mio
Bat Brin git to have
Stitches in his had .

Monday, March 24

I went to my nanny's
and Brian cut his head
and my Father cut
his toe with the
power-saw.
(Did your father have to have
stitches in his toe Shawn?) No.
But Brian got to have
stitches in his head.

Shawn is experimenting with a variety of conventions on this writing occasion. He uses capital letters for the day and month, for *I*, for names (*Brin, Father*), for the beginning of a sentence (*Bat*), and for important words (*Piwr-si*). He is also exploring a range of punctuation. He tries out apostrophes in *nie's* and *hi's* (observe the difference between these apostrophes and the comma in the date), has a period marking what could be the end of a sentence (*my Father cut hi's tow.*), and uses a hyphen in *Piwr-si*.

In the process of writing, Shawn has edited for spelling (*wnt* is changed to *went; miy* becomes *my* in the third line) and for handwriting (the backwards *B* in *Brin* is corrected at the end). His store of conventionally spelled words has enlarged; 63% of the words he uses in this journal entry are spelled conventionally, including the word *stitches* borrowed from the teacher's question. We can also see that Shawn's preferred vowel has shifted from *a* to *i* (*miy* for *my* as compared with *may* in February; *git* for *got* as compared with *gat* on March 11).

Thank you very much for bringing Chico
to school. It was fun to have her here!

7 May    May 6.

I Wiat fiuhing
lasnet and I cit
a fish and We alims
cit athr fish But
it gat awauy.
I Brag a raddit to
school and he is
nrvs. the End
a trot
What kind of fish did you catch Shawn?

May 7/May 6
I went fishing
last night and I caught
a fish and we almost
caught another fish but
it got away.
I brang (brought) a rabbit to
school and he is
nervous. The End
(What kind of fish did you catch Shawn?)
A trout.

In this entry we can see a consolidation of Shawn's writing efforts. Observe the evolution of the spelling of *fish* within this single text: from *fiuhing,* to *fish* with the *s* squeezed in, to a confident *fish* in line four. *School* is now spelled correctly and *raddit* has the appropriate appearance despite the reversed *b*'s. Shawn is now demonstrating a grasp of multi-syllable words: *lasnet* for *last night, alims* for *almost, athr* for *another, nrvs* for *nervous.* He is beginning many sentences with capital letters and ending them with periods. He has also decided that these journal entries are stories, hence *the End.*

June·10

Danielle·T is caming to
My hoes today and
Look four Sallamds
And Pot them in
My cawaeam and
we will Plaey in
the Plaeygrawb and
thein sey will go
home the Ead

June 10
Danielle T is coming to
my house today to
look for salamanders
and put them in
my aquarium, and
we will play in
the playground and
then she will go
home. The End

Throughout May and into June Shawn continues experimenting freely with his writing. The length of his journal entries has increased somewhat; they now average thirty-four words. During this time his spelling has become more and more conventional as well; an average of 72% of the words are spelled conventionally. Shawn continues to edit: *June* is corrected; *hoes* becomes *houes*; *then* becomes *thein*. He substitutes homophones: *four* for *for*. He is still playing with apostrophes: *sallamd's*. He is also still very comfortable spelling functionally: *cawaeam (aquarium)*; *sallamd's (salamander's)*. He is now playing with a new vowel (*pot* for *put*) and with complex vowels (*plaey* for *play*, *sey* for *she*). He is using capital letters at the beginning of lines and at the beginning of important words. Other than the apostrophe in *sallamd's* and two periods marking spaces, punctuation hasn't been important on this writing occasion.

My and my dad are
going    fishing    tonit
and    we    are    saing utl
9:00    and    I    am    going

to    fish    and than    I
will    go    home.

I hope you catch some more fish
tonight Shawn! Will you eat them
if you do? Yes

Me and my Dad are
going fishing tonight
and we are staying until
9:00 and I am going
to fish and then I
will go home.

This was Shawn's last journal entry for the year. We see him continuing his explorations (*9:00*), self-correcting (*My* is altered to *Me*), substituting words he knows how to spell (*than* for *then*), spelling functionally when necessary (*tonit, saing, utl*), beginning with a capital letter and ending with a period.

# Reflections

What do we learn about writing development from Shawn's journal writing? First we see the importance of experimentation and risk-taking. Shawn's development as a writer was dependent on his willingness to engage in the process. As long as he was concerned about what he perceived to be the constraints of writing in the classroom (learned from his experiences the previous year), he was unwilling to try to write on his own. The teacher, understanding his hesitation, accepted whatever he produced and continued to engage him in the sharing of meaning. Slowly her responses to the information offered in his writing persuaded Shawn that what counted was his message. Once he felt comfortable with that notion, he began taking risks, writing more freely, using many sources of knowledge and a range of strategies for producing text.

Although sometimes difficult to perceive, Shawn's intentions and his ability to organize his writing were well developed from the very beginning of the year. The meaning of his journal entries was always clear and concise and expressed grammatically. His difficulty resided in creating a surface representation for what he wanted to say. As Shawn gained experience as a writer, transcription became less of a problem for him. As he gained control over letter/sound relationships, as his sense of how words looked and his store of conventional spelling grew, his journal entries became more and more readable.

Shawn's journal writing also demonstrates the close interplay of reading and writing. In his first independent efforts we can see him reading to find words he wants to use and copying them. Later, as he becomes more of a risk-taker, his editing and self-correction reveal how he functions as a reader in the process of writing. The way in which his spelling becomes more and more conventional over time is a further reflection of the influence of reading on his writing development.

Perhaps the most important insight for me was the realization of what a complex orchestration each child's writing efforts represent. Each written product is the result of many different decisions: decisions about audience, topic, genre, layout, sentence structure, spelling and style. Even in his early independent writing Shawn demonstrated his ability to deal with all of these decisions in some way. Sometimes we can see him decide to disregard certain aspects of the process for the moment. His decision to spell functionally is that kind of decision; it reflects his placing meaning in a position of greater importance than convention.

As teachers, our fear might be that his decision to neglect common writing conventions for the present will lead to his never considering them, but that doesn't seem to be the case. As Shawn discovers the arbitrary conventions we use for transcribing meaning, we find them creeping into his writing: his spelling gradually becomes consistently more conventional; punctuation appears and is used more appropriately; his texts become both semantically and syntactically more complex; the overall organization of what he wants to write becomes more worked out. But not all of these developments proceed in a smooth, linear fashion. Shawn's journal writing illustrates how something he appeared to know is temporarily ignored as he experiments with some new aspect of the process that has caught his attention.

The clearest evidence we have of Shawn's ability to orchestrate the many aspects of writing are present in his self-corrections. These are instances where he changes his mind about something he has written. Perhaps he notices a letter incorrectly formed, or a misspelling; or he may decide he wants to change a particular word; maybe his head has got ahead of his hand and he recognizes he's left something out that he decides to insert. In each case Shawn is making decisions based on the meaning of what he's writing, coordinated with what he knows about conventional spelling, grammar, punctuation or genre.

Because writing requires attention to so many different kinds of information at the same time, writers cannot always use everything they know when they write. They must be free to decide what aspects of the writing process will engage their attention for the moment.

# Instructional Implications

### How can adults help children to communicate through written language?

My correspondence with Irene is an example of how we can invite children to share their writing with us. I initiated the use of written language as a way of communicating with Irene shortly after I met her (she was five and a half). On a blank piece of paper I wrote (I actually printed my message, saying the words as I printed them in case she wasn't yet able to read what I was writing) something like, 'Hello Irene, how are you today?' In this way I began a 'written conversation.' When I handed her the paper, she responded by telling me she couldn't write anything. I replied that I was sure she could write her name, which she did. When she handed me back the paper, I continued the conversation with another question, once more reading aloud what I was writing. Again she was reluctant to try writing anything on her own. I suggested that she 'pretend' to write and she could help me read what she had written. I was thus able to encourage her to write a little more, mainly letters of the alphabet, which she named as she wrote. I replied with meaningful messages about what she was writing.

Because of this interaction and subsequent ones, it was not surprising that Irene chose to use letters of the alphabet to represent what she wanted to say when she wrote to me in Indiana (page 15). I wrote to her on a number of other occasions and each time I received a reply — sometimes a picture with writing on it, sometimes just text. In the beginning of our sharing I was unable to read Irene's writing myself, but her mother would have her read the text and she, in turn, would read the message to me. In the case of the Indiana letter, her mother penciled on the back what Irene read to her. By the time I received the later 'Cabbagetown' letter I was familiar with the sorts of things that interested her and was able to read the text with little assistance (I did need help with 'Cabbagetown').

Just as we invite children to participate in oral language by talking to them, we can engage children in the exploration of written language by writing to and with them. We need to have paper and pencils, pens, crayons and markers readily at hand, and to use them in ways that invite children to participate with us in making meaning. How can we know what their messages say? In precisely the same way they find out what our writing is about. We read what we write to them and ask them to read what they write to us. In the process of exchanging meaning, they learn to understand our writing and we learn to read theirs.

## How can parents and teachers help children to discover the many functions of written language?

The examples of children's writing used in this book are illustrations of the many different ways children see written language being used: for making requests, giving instructions, conveying information, creating stories, making notices, explaining situations, describing experiences, writing letters, giving reminders, sharing feelings. None of the children whose writing I have presented were explicitly taught how to use their writing for these purposes. They learned from watching how the adults in their environment were using written language.

Obviously the answer to how we can help children discover the many uses of written language is to have them see us writing and to invite them into the process. Every time we allow children to watch us writing for some specific purpose we are inadvertently demonstrating how written language can be used. No formal teaching is necessary. If we write notices for the children to read, they too will write notices. If they see us writing memos and lists, they will write memos and lists for themselves — provided, of course, that we create situations in which such writing is seen to be useful and acceptable.

## Why should we encourage children to write by themselves from the very start?

Children learn to talk by talking. By participating in conversations, they receive feedback about what they have said. They discover whether their meaning has been understood. They discover the interactive effect of what they have tried to say through any confirmation or extension given. They also learn by listening to others talk. By eavesdropping on conversations, they receive demonstrations of language in action.

The crucial aspect of learning oral language, however, is having the opportunity of being a language user. This is equally important for learning about written language. It is only by trying to use written language themselves that children can figure out what does and what doesn't matter. Our role in the process is to respond to the intentions that underlie each writing effort. That isn't always easy to do, particularly when we are used to correcting printing, spelling, punctuation and grammatical errors. When we respond only to these surface aspects of text, we are actually saying to children that we consider meaning to be unimportant. I'm not suggesting that we should never help children attend to conventions; conventions are necessary. But they must not supplant meaning as the focus of writing. The need for conventions comes into play when writing is to be published — that is, if a piece is to be turned into a book or to appear in the school or class newspaper. But not every piece of writing a child does either needs to be or should be examined for how well the conventions have been used.

### What is the value of having children keep a journal?

For Shawn's teacher journal writing served several purposes. Her primary reason for using it was that it gave her the chance every day to have some personal reading and writing time with each child. It let her 'eavesdrop' on the children's experiences and learn about what was happening to them outside the classroom. She dialogued with them through their journals, writing her responses in their presence to demonstrate how written language is related to meaning. She often used the words the children spelled functionally, both to ensure that she would be able to read what they had written at some later date, and to juxtapose for the children the conventional and functional spellings. Occasionally the children would notice her conventional spelling, but usually they accepted it without comment. After writing her entries, she encouraged the children to read them back to her, and in this way observed how their reading was developing.

The daily journal, then, is full of learning potential for both children and teachers. Children have the opportunity of writing every day and of receiving almost immediate feedback on the meaning of what they have written. Teachers have the opportunity of observing children in the process of developing as readers and writers. There are many ways journals may be used. Some teachers may choose to leave them for essentially private writing, responding only when requested to. Others may decide to keep them strictly private, never responding at all. There are, however, two rules that must not be violated: journal writing should be daily, and the writing must never be marked for neatness and/or spelling. The purpose of a journal is to allow children a chance to explore ideas and the writing process without restriction.

### What have we learned from our examination of children's writing?

We've seen, I think, the need to look beyond neatness and accuracy. We've begun to recognize the experimenting that occurs whenever children write, to understand what their 'mistakes' reveal about their knowledge of the writing process.

We can draw several important implications for classroom practice from our observations. Our experiences with all aspects of language are cumulative. Experiences with written language enhance our ability to interact with and create oral language; oral language provides resources for generating written language. Because the vehicle for language development is language itself, we must create an environment which provides opportunities for reading and writing. That means that children need to read many different kinds of writing in order to learn the diverse forms writers use for presenting their ideas. They need access to books both factual and fictional, to magazines, newspapers, pamphlets, notices and letters. It also means that children need to write. They need to write for many different purposes. They need to write on topics of their own choosing. They need to write for real audiences — for themselves, for both younger and older children, for adults they know, and for some general unknown audience as well.

The environment we create must be one in which children will want to write. This means, first and foremost, allowing them to be owners of their own work. Children must feel comfortable exploring written language in whatever ways interest them. They need to decide what they will write about, what they will say about it, and how much attention they will pay to conventions at any particular time. Children can become writers only by learning to make these kinds of decisions for themselves, and that requires experimentation. Every time we set the topic, ask for a particular rhetorical form, expect accurate spelling and punctuation to take precedence over meaning, or correct 'errors,' we take away text ownership. We take away opportunities for experimenting with the writing process.

Learning to read and write is a process of experiencing language. There is no end-product. Fluency is not some state that is finally attained; we are all continually arriving. Writing develops in many directions at once. It develops continually, sometimes inconspicuously, sometimes in dramatic spurts. Eventually, as the various conventions are mastered, children develop a common fund of concepts, but the point of entry and the path of progress are different for each child. Consequently, writing development needs encouragement and support, not a carefully sequenced program. Each learner must discover the strategies that allow him or her to be a successful language user.

Children don't need to be told how to write; they need to be shown.

Writing involves a constant sharing with others, talking and writing about ideas and getting feedback on whether those ideas have worked or not. In order to help children to develop as writers, we need to share in the writing process by being writers ourselves. By providing demonstrations of writing in action, by being partners in the creating process, we do more to help children figure out how to be writers themselves than all of our correcting of their 'mistakes' can ever hope to accomplish.

We need to understand how we either limit or enhance development by the experiences we set for children. Activities that involve fragments of language, that discourage children from taking chances, that don't permit the exchanging of ideas, can only serve to make reading and writing more difficult. It is by creating natural language environments in which children are enthusiastically experimenting with written language that we can help them become comfortable and successful writers.

**There are some guiding principles:**

● We need to place meaning at the forefront of learning about written language.

● We need to accept the fact that development takes place on many fronts at the same time.

● We need to understand the importance of experimentation and risk-taking in the process of learning to write.

● We need to support children's experiments, watching for conventions as they creep into their writing.

● We need to recognize the importance of having audiences respond to the meaning of what children have written.

● We need to provide demonstrations of what is involved in being a writer.

We must try to understand what the children are trying to do and then help them do it. But in order to understand what they are trying to do, we must also discover language for ourselves. It is only by observing language in use, by watching language users, that our own understanding of language can grow. And it is only from such understanding that we will be able to make curricular decisions that better match the children's intuitions about how language works.